A Guide for New Genealogists
DISCOVERING YOUR ROOTS

22 Steps

In
Researching
Your Family Tree

DARRELL GIBBS

22 Steps In Researching Your Family Tree

Email: darrell.gibbs56@outlook.com
Website: darrellgibbs-author.com

Available Amazon
ISBN: 978-1-9808596-6-6 (Paperback)
ISBN: 978-0-9959550-6-6 (Electronic book)

EBook Version also available:
•   On Smashwords at
    https://www.smashwords.com/books/view/815440
    ISBN: 978-1-3701847-9-8 (Smashwords ePub Version)

And Draft2Digital at https://www.books2read.com/u/31MzaW

I dedicate this book to all genealogists seeking answers to their ancestral beginnings.

DISCLAIMER - ANCESTRAL RESEARCH

Genealogies are always a work in progress. Due to the nature of this e-book and potential human error, I cannot guarantee the information is 100% accurate. Every effort has been made to ensure that the quality of material presented is for the beginner genealogist. The information presented is a place for you to find clues and information for your own research. References throughout this e-book should be checked for accuracy and validity. Mistakes are made by all of us, especially early record keepers. The information has been assembled in good faith. I have tried my best to create a good source document for all family historians.

If you have any comments, concerns, or questions regarding the information presented, please contact me.

darrell.gibbs56@outlook.com

ACKNOWLEDGMENTS

I would like to thank Linda Bogert who has put up with me in getting this e-book finished. Genealogy takes a tremendous amount time and is an addictive consuming hobby. Researching for endless hours and writing this project has definitely taken me away from spending valuable and precious time with such a beautiful and caring woman.

Table of Contents

CHAPTER ONE

The 22 Steps

INTRODUCTION TO THE 22 STEPS

When you start about family, about lineage and ancestry, you are talking about every person on earth." Alex Haley – Author of 'Roots: The Saga of an American Family'

This book is for new genealogists who plan on researching their own family tree[1]. Inside this book there are the necessary steps that you should take when you research. It is jam packed with lots of information and web links for you to start your genealogy research to begin your family tree.

Genealogy – What is it? You might ask yourself. And then you wonder, how do I start researching my family tree? Or, why should I research my genealogy? And, what will I get out of it? Genealogy is a family history tracing your lineage and ancestral history.

These are all excellent questions. Throughout this book, if you follow the step-by-step procedure you will gain the knowledge and tools to research your ancestors effectively.

I will pass on the steps, important facts and website links so you can further your knowledge and research your family tree to reach that goal. This is an informative guide with the necessary tools to make you become an efficient genealogist to help you find facts about your ancestors. Through your research following this guide you will have an awesome family tree to share with your family.

You are probably like millions of other people around the world who are curious about finding out where your ethnic and cultural backgrounds came from. You have come to the right place in your quest to help guide you in your search of your own unique genealogy background.

A few years ago I was probably just like you as I didn't know where to start unless I was talking or getting information from my mother. The Internet is now a very valuable resource. Anyone with a computer and the Internet can get information on their ancestors if they know where to look.

The aim of this book is to pass on the tools I feel will help you in achieving your goals in finding out more about your ancestors.

Researching your family tree may be a hobby or a passion but it will

---

1   *Family Tree or a Pedigree Chart – a diagram that displays different people and family members and their relationships over several generations of a family. It is also called a genealogical tree.*

consume your life and become an addiction. After all, if you seek answers, having a starting point and set of guidelines to follow will help you to achieve your goals.

Reaching those goals all depends on your thirst for family ancestral knowledge. Your curiosity and dedication in finding those answers await to be discovered through your hours research.

If you are beginner genealogist and are starting your family tree from scratch then the best way to start is with yourself and then work back in time. Look in the mirror and start your quest. You will definitely get some personal enjoyment and achieve personal satisfaction while uncovering facts of your ancestors. You will learn some very interesting details about where they came from and how they lived their lives.

Alfred the Great was a famous and well-known Anglo-Saxon king during the 9th Century in England. King Alfred was the king of Wessex and Danish Mercia. Alfred's genealogy and ancestry has been well documented over the last thousand years. He was a smart monarch who promoted universal literacy and recorded everything in the Anglo-Saxon Chronicles (ASC). King Alfred had many of the church clergy and monks transcribe events into the ASC. Some of the information can and have been misleading as to their authenticity and accuracy. The scribes of these chronicles may not have been entirely truthful in their writings as they may have exaggerated a little bit. There is still some debate among genealogists and scholars about the data but at least there is a record to work from.

As you research your family tree, find documents with relevant data of your ancestors. Record the information you researched into a log or a journal. Keep a separate journal on each family researched to help you as you work on your family tree. I would suggest to colour code each log or journal that you use to identify each individual family unit.

Initiate your online family tree to research your ancestors on genealogy websites such as Ancestry[2], MyHeritage[3] or FindMyPast[4]. I would start with a *Free Membership* first.

You will gain more skills and tools as you progress on your family tree. As you become more familiar with the website gathering information on your tree upgrade to a *Paid Subscription* to have access to more tools and features on the site.

---

2   www.Ancestry.com

3   www.MyHeritage.com

4   www.findmypast.com

Wouldn't it be awesome to leave a personal legacy of your heritage to your grandchildren and future generations?

Genealogy resources on the Internet are mind boggling and can be quite over-whelming in your search. You should formulate an action plan and execute it so that you can reach your overall goal. That goal is to put together a professional looking family tree. Tracing your family tree starts where you should follow a guideline or a set of rules. Each family search is different but you can follow the same steps for each family that you research.

Inside this book I will guide you pointing you in the right direction during your search following a step-by-step procedure. During each step you will have website links to use while you research your family tree for gathering facts of family members.

Steps to start your journey are quite simple. Researching your family roots can be quite time consuming and can take years to complete. Is there someone in your family who has already started your family tree. Gather whatever information you can from you're living relatives and use the information that has already been started.

Get the proper documentation for the information you researched and the proper source citation. Search the Internet, church records, obituaries, historical and genealogical societies in the area where your ancestor lived. Become a member of an online Ancestry Group to reach out during your search. Once you do that — research another family member. Keep repeating the process over and over again until you think your done. The ancestry wheel keeps turning as you discover more facts as they unfold.

At a certain point in your research you might want to create and write a book about your family tree to leave as a keepsake. Something left in your legacy to pass down to your children and grandchildren.

Have you started a family tree or are you unsure of where to start? Are you still working on a tree? If you haven't started your family tree that's okay. You can start by using my checklist for the steps that I've learned in my research.

THE 22 STEPS - CHECKLIST

22 Steps in Researching Your Family Tree

Below are the "22 Steps in Researching Your Family Tree" a checklist I use for my own genealogy research.

1. Start with yourself
2. Gather what information you already have or know
3. Start the search with one family at a time by talking to family members and relatives
4. Become a member of an online ancestry website
5. Join an online Genealogy forum
6. Obtain or locate copies of birth certificates or baptism records, marriage records, death or burial records and obituary notices
7. Find ancestors in Census Records, Military documents and ship's passenger lists
8. Find ancestors through city directories, land records, court and prison records, and in immigration & naturalization records
9. Contact other relatives and descendants through ancestry website or Genealogy forum
10. Join a mailing list and search message boards through RootWeb
11. Expand your family history resources and use social media (Facebook and Twitter) to make new connections
12. Read genealogy articles
13. Research online newspaper archives
14. Check websites that offer historical or genealogical societies in the area you're researching
15. Subscribe to a free newsletter or a blog
16. Check out funeral home records
17. Check out online cemetery records and visit them, record and take photographs of your findings

18. Go to locations where your ancestors came from

19. Re-evaluate your research and ensure everything is well documented with reference citations

20. Create your own Family Tree Record Sheets and Pedigree Charts

21. Backup your personal or online files onto a USB flash drive and properly label it

22. Share and publish your family tree

Download the "22 Steps To Help You In Your Journey For Researching Your Family Tree"[5] to your computer. These steps will help you in researching your family tree. Keep them close by and refer to them in your quest for your family tree.

---

5 Download the "22 Steps..." https://darrellgibbs-author.com/wp-content/uploads/2017/10/22-Steps-To-Help-You-In-Your-Journey-For-Researching-Your-Family-Tree-1.pdf

NOTES

CHAPTER TWO

Steps 1 – 2 – 3

INTRO TO FIRST THREE STEPS

Years ago my mother started our family tree. I was fascinated to learn more about our ancestral history. I regret not taking genealogy as seriously as I should have. If I had of, I think I would have had a better understanding of genealogy research today.

If you are new to genealogy and just starting your family tree then you now have a great resource and tool to help you in researching your ancestors. One aim of this book is to point you in the right direction as you start your research.

Anyone who wants to start a family tree today need to do extensive research on family members and the Internet has a lot of resources available. New genealogists also need to follow a step-by-step format or guideline getting as much information as they can on their ancestors.

The Internet is an awesome tool for you to start your research and this self-help guide is now your newest desktop companion.

In the last chapter I outlined the steps I learned and follow as I do my own family tree research. The book is broken down into chapters with separate steps so that you can concentrate on your own comprehensive and detailed research.

In this chapter the steps we will go over are:

1. Start with yourself

2. Gather what information you already have or know

3. Start the search with one family at a time by talking to family members and relatives

Wouldn't it be awesome to leave a legacy of your heritage to your grandchildren and future generations.

All right! Lets get our *'genealogy ball caps'* on, paper and pen in hand, let's begin...

STEP 1

Start With Yourself

Look in the mirror — gather all information about yourself:

- birth or baptismal certificate
- old photographs
- newspapers or clippings
- certificates or diplomas
- marriage certificate
- Reports
- a biography
- anything else that you may think that is noteworthy

STEP 2

Gather What Information You Already Have or Know

Start your research by writing everything down on paper before inputting the information into a genealogy program or an online genealogy website.

Keep a neat and legible document. Record all the info you have into a journal with pencil. Use a pencil instead of a pen so you can make any necessary corrections later on. Transcribe the information as a handwritten record onto forms, into a journal or download and complete a computerized form such as a Research Log[6]. This will be a good source document for future reference in your journal or file.

If you prefer, use a computer program such as Microsoft OneNote[7]. The program can be used across all platforms (Windows, Apple and Android). If you don't have an online genealogy program to input information into I would suggest to go to Erin Williamson Klein's website, My Family History Files[8] she has an excellent OneNote template for recording your ancestry. The OneNote file has all the necessary forms for your family tree.

If you have a Hotmail or an Outlook account you can setup OneNote online for free.

Gather all the information that you have of your parents, siblings, grandparents, aunts, uncles and your cousins. Collect and organize all photographs and certificates. Write down all you can about your ancestors.Scan or make photocopies of anything you already have to work with and store your originals in a safe place.

- Download a Pedigree Chart[9]

- Family Group Record Sheet[10]

- or use the OneNote template[11] I previously suggested above.

---

6   *Research Log -*
    http://www.cs.williams.edu/~bailey/genealogy/index_files/ResearchRecordSheet.pdf
7   *Microsoft OneNote - https://www.onenote.com/*
8   *My Family History Files – Microsoft OneNote Template -*
    http://myfamilyhistoryfiles.com/onenote-a-to-z/
9   *Pedigree Chart - http://misbach.org/download/pedigree_chart.pdf*
10 *Family Group Record Sheet - http://misbach.org/download/FamilyGroupRecord.pdf*
11 *Use OneNote template - https://www.onenote.com/*

You can even create your own if you'd like. Use whatever forms you feel you would like to use in your research project.

Use the sheets to document the information you already have on your family and ancestors. The data you have now is your initial research info about your family and relatives. Record any information you have collected through your online research.

STEP 3

Start The Search With One Family At A Time By Talking To Family Members And Relatives

Download a Correspondence Record Sheet[12] to record your contacts. Anyone that you get in contact with should be entered onto the sheet. Keep a correspondence sheet or a log as you setup your interviews to speak to your family and relatives.

Contact family members and relatives in your search by telephoning, mailing or emailing them and conduct an interview.

Interview each person that you get in contact with and ask a series or a list of questions that will help you fill in the blanks on your Family Record Sheet. If you contact a relative, you can either record it by audio or video (make sure you get their permission).

Get any vintage photographs and documents from relatives so that they can be scanned and digitized. Remember to log everything you receive and record the item from who you received it from.

Conduct your interview with a pre-planned printed list of questions. Select at least twenty-five questions. The more information you have about your ancestors the more detailed your research will be.

A good source of questions to ask during your interview can be viewed at DesertNews.com. They have an excellent article list titled 'Genealogy: 150 questions to ask family members about their lives[13]' by Barry Ewell, use it as a guide and reference. Select and create your own list of questions to ask during your interview.

Start with your own family first, remember to always work backwards when you are doing any family research.

Conduct the interviews either by telephone or visit them to make it more intimate. Visiting your relatives is a better approach as you will get more information that you otherwise wouldn't get.

---

12 *Correspondence Record Sheet -*
http://www.cs.williams.edu/~bailey/genealogy/index_files/CorrespondenceRecordSheet.pd f

13 *Genealogy: 150 questions to ask family members about their lives -*
https://www.deseretnews.com/article/865595932/Genealogy-150-questions-to-ask-family-members-about-their-lives.html

Download a basic Family Record Sheet[14] so that you can record any information on a family when you are conducting your research. This form is used to record important information such as given names, family surname, date and place born, date/place died and buried, father, mother, spouse's and marriage information and their children's information.

Keep this process going and complete the data for a number of families on separate sheets.

Next, you should create or download a Pedigree Chart. Once you have a number of Family Records Sheets completed you can start filling in your Pedigree Chart. Again, record all information you discover on a Research Log[15], citing any references you find.

The record sheets and charts in this book are just a few of the ones that you can download on the Internet. You can use these ones and tailor them to your needs or research for other ones and download. Use whatever ones you feel would be best used for your Family Tree.

Get the proper documentation for the source information you uncover. The information needs to be properly cited on what you find. Ensure you write it down; log and record it.

At a certain point in your research you might want to create and write a book about your family tree to leave as a keepsake. Something left in your legacy to pass down to your children and grandchildren.

In the next chapter the steps covered are:

Step 4 - Become a member of an online ancestry website

Step 5 - Join an online Genealogy forum

---

14 *Family Record Sheet - http://misbach.org/download/FamilyGroupRecord.pdf*

15 *Research Log -*
   http://www.cs.williams.edu/~bailey/genealogy/index_files/ResearchRecordSheet.pdf

NOTES

CHAPTER THREE

Steps 4 – 5

EARLY GENEALOGY

Grandchildren are a grandparent's link to the future. Grandparents are the child's link to the past." - Unknown Author

Genealogy isn't a new fad today as our ancestors and ancient civilizations have been recording family lineages for thousands of years.

Before the Internet, people around the world who researched their family trees had to rely on their parents and grandparents in getting that information. Family trees were passed down from generation to generation.

Information like old documents or articles, small trinkets, articles in old shoe boxes and cedar chests were stored throughout the house for safe keeping. Information stored in the home may have been in newspaper clippings, handwritten pieces of paper, inside the family bible or in old ledgers, documents like military records, birth and death certificates, etc.

Ancient civilizations used ingenious methods of keeping records and passed them down throughout the generations from one family to the next.

Before the discovery and invention of the written word, records were probably kept by the eldest family member who meticulously tied knots on a rope with other objects.

Why did different cultures tie knots the way they did? Individual groups did it for identifying different events or meanings. Knots were tied in different fashions and colours in a detailed methodology which had baffled archaeologists at one time. Archaeologists are understanding more about the different cultures as they piece together how and why they did it a certain way.

Early Vikings did not write down their sagas (stories) as they recited and memorized them passing them down to their children. We would call them stories but they are known as sagas. Vikings would sit around the mead halls while skalds and storytellers would recite their sagas of epic battles during wars and other adventures in poems, stories and songs. The skalds and storytellers described sagas of a family or a person as the saga came alive praising their lords and kings. The skalds recited the sagas of their Viking warlords of their historical tales and deeds.

The Chinese on the other hand are the true masters of genealogy. They kept detailed genealogical written records of clan and branch genealogies of family records or annals. In China it is a tradition that only male names are recorded in the family book and many Chinese families still keep the books that are thousands of years old. The earliest known record dates back to around 1500 BC when they inscribed family trees on turtle shells and cow bones.

Are you interested in finding out how many ancestors you have had over the past 500 years? A chart depicting how many ancestors we have had on the next page called Theoretical Number of Ancestors can be used as a quick reference. Look at the data on the chart for the amount of potential ancestors you would have over the last eighteen generations if there was no cross-linking of any of our ancestors, the information is staggering.

THEORETICAL NUMBER OF ANCESTORS (No Cross-Linking)

18 GENERATIONS

15th Great Grandparents	131,072
14th Great Grandparents	65,536
13th Great Grandparents	32,768
12th Great Grandparents	16,384
11th Great Grandparents	8,192
10th Great Grandparents	4,096
9th Great Grandparents	2,048
8th Great Grandparents	1,024
7th Great Grandparents	512
6th Great Grandparents	256
5th Great Grandparents	128
4th Great Grandparents	64
3rd Great Grandparents	32
2nd Great Grandparents	16
Great Grandparents	8
Grandparents	4
Parents	2
Self	0

Total Number of Ancestors in
18 Generations   262,144

Reference RootsWeb.com

An excellent article to read that explains the chart very well can be assessed on the RootsWeb[16] website.

Having ancient family records or a unique turtle shell that told a story and traced your family tree back three thousand years ago would be an unbelievable family treasure. A genealogist would think that they had just discovered a new priceless gem. That gem would hold the key to your past.

Wouldn't it be awesome to leave a personal legacy of your heritage to your grandchildren and future generations?

Getting old information reminds me of the TV Show 'American Pickers'. The hosts of the program, Mike Wolfe and Frank Fritz, travel around the United States looking for unique antique items for their collections, businesses and potential buyers.

Mike and Frank go to different locations across the US hoping to find a one of a kind antique item searching in people's homes or buildings. Every item they find tells us a unique story and they document it very well on the show. They research and take pictures of the items so that the viewer watching the show gets to see video or pictures, detailed information and the history of the item. It is interesting how they get their point across and the show is very entertaining.

That's what we have to do when researching our genealogy. We have to create a saga about what we find so that our descendants have an excellent family story to tell and pass on.

The point I can't stress enough is recording our finds when we do our research so that the information is properly documented in an orderly fashion.

The information that each family historian finds in the documents, certificates and photos we discover needs proper citation. Each item we find tells a story from our ancestors past and each one is a treasure for our journals or record sheets.

Each document or sheet you complete for your family tree needs to tell a story. Get as much information as you can.

In Chapter 2, I talked about the first three steps to take when doing your own research. The next two steps are:

Step 4 – Become a member of an online ancestry website

Step 5 – Join an online Genealogy forum

---

16 *RootsWeb website -*
    http://freepages.genealogy.rootsweb.ancestry.com/~harringtonfamilies/110_part2.htm

So, now you have the "genealogy bug". You've checked in all the nooks and crannies of your attic and basement and interviewed some of your relatives about your ancestors. Now's the time to dig deeper into your tree researching your grandparents, aunts and uncles. Remember to get documented proof of only one family member at a time and then work on that family. Input the data into your Family Record Sheet. Getting as much information on your ancestors will be rewarding in the long run.

You should really become a member of an online ancestry website and join an online genealogy forum. As a member of these sites you will be able to increase and have more resources to conduct your research. Your reward will come two-fold becoming a member of these forums.

Listen, research, read, learn, document, participate, ask questions and share.

STEP 4

Become a member of an Online Ancestry Website

During this step you should first consider what features and support that you will receive once you become a member of an online ancestry website. Compare different genealogy websites to see what is available and what they offer. Weigh the pro's and con's of each one before you make the final decision.

Learn as much as you can about the website. Do they provide you with help files, tutorials and videos so that you can efficiently use their search features? On the websites try other search methods in finding your ancestors, you will be surprised of the hints you will receive. Remember the search method you used and try it again with your next ancestral search. Don't leave any stone unturned, try everything you can possibly think of and record your findings.

If you are just beginning your Family Tree, start first with a free account even though you'll have limited accessibility. It is a good starting point to learn from and then use the different search features on the website you signed up with. Most online sites will have a trial period with an option for you to purchase a subscription later on as you search.

You want the best online genealogy website available so I would recommend reading the information at TopTenReviews called 'The Best Genealogy Search Services'[17] by Renee Shipley. Renee takes the top nine websites breaking down each site and compares them. Using the information from these comparisons will save you a lot research time.

The information provided is very detailed with an overall rating and bar-graph to help you make your final selection. It will enable you to make a positive decision and then you can select the website you would like to become a member with.

---

17 *'The Best Genealogy Search Services' by Renee Shipley -*
   http://www.toptenreviews.com/services/home/best-genealogy-websites/

You can compare the top three yourself by clicking on the links in the footnotes below:

- Ancestry.com[18] (14-day Free Trial / US Discovery package $99 for six months after trial)

- MyHeritage.com[19] (Premium Membership a 1-year Subscription $82.50 good for 2500 people)

- FamilySearch.org[20] - Free Account - nonprofit family history organization

- Family Tree Magazine has an awesome article called Best Genealogy Websites[21] check it out.

There is a drop-down box where you can sort by category by selecting from 16 different categories. Some of the categories you can select from are:

- The Best European Genealogy Websites

- The Best Family Tree and Sharing Websites

- Best Websites for Immigrant Research

It is an excellent resource page, it will help you make a decision for what website you would like to use in your research.

18 Ancestry.com (14-day Free Trial / US Discovery package $99 for six months after trial)
    http://www.ancestry.com/cs/offers/freetrial
19 MyHeritage.com (Premium Membership a 1-year Subscription $82.50 good for 2500
    people) http://www.myheritage.com/paywall
20 FamilySearch.org - Free Account - nonprofit family history organization -
    https://www.familysearch.org
21 Best Genealogy Websites - https://www.familytreemagazine.com/best-genealogy-websites/

STEP 5

Join An Online Genealogy Forum

Why should you join an online genealogy forum?

Joining an online genealogy forum is an excellent communication method for you to share and exchange a vast amount of information. You can connect with other genealogy enthusiasts who are like minded in researching. You will be able to connect with long lost relatives, learn from them, improve your research skills, be able to exchange and share information with them.

There are many reasons to join an online message board, a bulletin board or a forum. It opens up past hidden doors that were once closed to you revealing genealogy tools and resources that will assist you in your quest.

Some excellent resources for online message boards to begin your search are:

- In the US - try the Federation of Genealogical Societies[22]
- In the UK, the British Genealogy & Family History Forums[23]
- In Canada, CanGenealogy[24]

Another informative website is AncestralFindings[25], it has one web page called the Genealogy Gold Podcast page.

On this page there are currently 150 podcasts that you can select and listen to. You can even download them as there is a wide variety of ancestry topics to select from to learn. You also have the option of joining and subscribing to the website on iTunes, YouTube, RSS and Google Play so that you can listen to them. One interesting episode that you might find interesting is podcast 36, AF-036: Online Resources for Researching Your Scottish Ancestors, you could apply these methods in your research.

---

22 *Federation of Genealogical Societies - https://fgs.org/*

23 *British Genealogy & Family History Forums - https://www.british-genealogy.com/*

24 *CanGenealogy - http://www.cangenealogy.com/*

25 *AncestralFindings - Genealogy Gold Podcast page - https://ancestralfindings.com/genealogygold/*

If you're interested in what types of libraries there are for genealogy research, read the article 'The Different Types of Libraries Used in Genealogical Research, and Their Unique Values[26]'.

While researching don't always believe what you research, I can't stress it enough, make sure that you record all documents and cite the reference of your genealogy find. Also, make sure that the source is reliable.

Doing online research on your family tree will definitely take up a lot of your time. A lot of websites do offer you free services and resources while some offer you a lot more for a paid subscription or membership.

Do your research on the genealogy websites, and forums; select one and get the best bang for your buck!

In the next chapter the following steps will be covered:

Step 6 - Obtain or locate copies of birth certificates or baptism records, marriage records, death or burial records and obituary notices

Step 7 - Find ancestors in Census Records, Military documents and ship's passenger lists

Step 8 - Find ancestors through city directories Land records, court & prison records and in immigration & naturalization record

Step 9 - Contact other relatives and descendants through ancestry website or Genealogy forum

---

26 *The Different Types of Libraries Used in Genealogical Research, and Their Unique Values - https://ancestralfindings.com/the-different-types-of-libraries-used-in-genealogical-research-and-their-unique-values/*

NOTES

CHAPTER FOUR

Steps 6 – 7 – 8 – 9

DOCUMENTING YOUR RESEARCH

Our family bloodlines and roots are like an acorn beneath the majestic white oak tree. The acorn doesn't fall too far from the tree to begin new offspring. Those results are our children to carry on our inherited family legacy.

Last chapter we covered steps 4 & 5 for you to take in your family research, they were:

Step 4 - Become a member of an online ancestry website

Step 5 - Join an online Genealogy forum

Obtaining documented proof for your family tree is very important. As a genealogist, you want to narrow your searches of the person you are researching to get accurate data for your tree. Record your findings and log it into your journal. Getting that information can be very rewarding if you know where to search.

The next four steps to help in researching your family tree are:

Step 6 - Obtain or locate copies of birth certificates or baptism records, marriage records, death or burial records and obituary notices.

Step 7 - Find ancestors in Census Records, Military documents and ship's passenger lists

Step 8 - Find ancestors through city directories, land records, court & prison records and in immigration & naturalization records

Step 9 - Contact other relatives and descendants through ancestry website or Genealogy forum

During these steps it will seem like you are diving off a high rock cliff into the depths of a bottomless ocean. Set your fears aside and roll up your sleeves. Your thirst of knowledge for your ancestors will slowly get uncovered.

The more you research, the more information you will want to get on each family member or ancestor. Your ancestors' secrets will begin to unravel because your inner detective skills reveal hard documentary evidence. Some of the data you discover will surprise or maybe even shock you. Overall, you will see positive results of your tree.

If you do it right and record everything that you find in a professional, meticulous and a systematic format, you will have an excellent family tree to be proud of.

STEP 6

Obtain or locate copies of birth certificates or baptism records, marriage records, death or burial records and obituary notices

During this step you may already have a copy of a birth, marriage or death certificate, record the information into your journal or the record sheet.

If you start a family tree with an online genealogy website such as Ancestry.com[27] the information will be saved in your tree. In Canada, for example, you can initiate searches for Birth, Marriage & Death on Ancestry.ca[28] for records of family members that you are researching and then go from there.

In the US, search for relatives on Archives.com (part of Ancestry.com) to 'Discover Your Ancestors'[29].

Search the various records from birth, marriage records, family trees and census records. There are newspaper records from 342,396,505 pages from 6,100+ newspapers dating back to 1700s— to the 2000s and a surname history. You can now join free for 14 days and then you will be charged $9.99 per month.

Check the obituary notices on online newspaper websites such as Newspapers.com[30], GenealogySA[31] or GenealogyBank[32].

If you are researching ancestors in the US try the USA Birth, Marriage & Death [33]record search which includes the Parish records on Ancestry.com.

---

27 *Ancestry.com - https://www.ancestry.com/*

28 *Canada - Birth, Marriage & Death - https://search.ancestry.ca/search/category.aspx?
    cat=34*

29 *Archives.com (part of Ancestry.com) to 'Discover Your Ancestors' -
    http://www.archives.com/GA.aspx?
    _act=ancestorSearch&utm_content=300x250_ancestry_historical_records&cam=3854&
    utm_campaign=300x250&tid=300x250_ancestry_historical_records&utm_source=Ances
    try.com&utm_medium=Advertising&hardcopycert=1*

30 *Newspapers.com - https://www.newspapers.com/*

31 *GenealogySA - https://www.genealogysa.org.au/resources/online-databases.html*

32 *GenealogyBank - https://www.genealogybank.com/explore/all-obits*

33 *USA Birth, Marriage & Death record on Ancestry.com -
    https://search.ancestry.co.uk/Places/US/Default.aspx?category=34&ldf=2*

Another website to try is FindMyPast[34] for birth and marriage records. The website also has a free search feature[35] as well.

During any search, try to use the free search websites first and see what you uncover about people you are researching. After searching the free sites, subscribe to a paid subscription website to get more information as you will have access to more searches.

In Canada, a great place to search for vital statistics is at the Library and Archives Canada for 'Births, Marriages and Deaths'[36] that have been recorded in Canada.

Other places to search are with Genealogical Societies and local cemeteries in the area your family resided. Local resources would be available and they can advise you where to narrow your search. There are also numerous online cemetery websites that you can search for where your ancestors may have been buried.

Links to various Genealogical Societies and cemeteries can be found at:

- Library and Archives Canada, Genealogy and Family History[37]
- United States Genealogy & Historical Society Directory[38]
- Genealogy Societies[39]
- RootsWeb Mailing Lists[40]
- Find A Grave[41]
- Cemetery Records Online at Interment.net[42]
- CanadaGenWeb's Cemetery Project[43]

---

34 FindMyPast - https://www.findmypast.com/articles/world-records/full-list-of-united-states-records/birth-marriage-and-death

35 The free search feature at FindMyPast - https://www.findmypast.com/free-ancestry-records

36 Library and Archives Canada for 'Births, Marriages and Deaths' that have been recorded in Canada - https://www.bac-lac.gc.ca/eng/discover/vital-statistics-births-marriages-deaths/births-marriages-deaths-recorded/Pages/births-marriages-deaths-recorded.aspx

37 Library and Archives Canada, Genealogy and Family History - http://www.bac-lac.gc.ca/eng/discover/genealogy/Pages/introduction.aspx

38 United States Genealogy & Historical Society Directory - http://www.censusfinder.com/genealogy-society-directory.htm

39 Genealogy Societies   http://www.archives.com/genealogy/free-societies.html

40 RootsWeb Mailing Lists - https://mailinglists.rootsweb.ancestry.com/listindexes/

41 Find A Grave - http://www.findagrave.com/

42 Cemetery Records Online at Interment.net — www.interment.net/

43 CanadaGenWeb's Cemetery Project   http://cemetery.canadagenweb.org/

- In Australia, you might want to try joining the website Genealogy SA[44] or Family Search - South Australia, Australia Online Genealogy Records[45] for your searches.

44 *GenealogySA Online Database Search -*
https://www.genealogysa.org.au/resources/online-databases.html
45 *FamilySearch South Australia, Australia Online Genealogy Records -*
https://www.familysearch.org/wiki/en/South_Australia,_Australia_Online_Genealogy_Rec
ords

STEP 7

Find ancestors in Census Records, Military documents and ship's passenger lists

As you make progress in your research verify what you have uncovered, substantiate and backup your proof for the person you are working on in your search. Continue with your research by finding facts through your country's census records.

Census records and sources to check out for your ancestors:

- USA – Ancestry.com[46], Archives.com[47], USGenWeb[48], MyHeritage.com[49]

- UK - UK Census Search Online[50], The National Archives[51], FreeCEN[52], RootsUK[53]

- Canada – Ancestry.ca[54], AncestralFindings.com[55], Library and Archives Canada[56]

- Australia – Ancestry.com.au[57], FamilySearch.org[58], National Archives of Australia[59]

---

46 *Census and Voter Lists on Ancestry.com — https:// search.ancestry.com/search/category.aspx?cat=35*

47 *Archives.com — create a FREE account to begin your search online — http://www.archives.com/member/*

48 *US Federal Census Research USGenWeb - http://www.us-census.org/research/index.html*

49 *MyHeritage.com - http://MyHeritage.com/*

50 *UK Census Search Online - https://www.ukcensusonline.com/*

51 *The National Archives – http://www.nationalarchives.gov.uk/help-with-your-research/research-guides/census-records/*

52 *FreeCEN UK Census Online - https://www.freecen.org.uk/*

53 *RootsUK – https://rootsuk.com/search/advanced/census/main/*

54 *Ancestry.ca — https://search.ancestry.ca/*

55 *AncestralFindings.com - https://ancestralfindings.com/first-time-user/*

56 *Censuses - Library and Archives Canada - http://www.bac-lac.gc.ca/eng/census/Pages/census.aspx*

57 *Australian Census Records - Ancestry.com.au - https://search.ancestry.com.au/search/group/AUSCENSUS? geo_a=r&geo_s=au&geo_t=au&geo_v=2.0.0&o_iid=41020&o_lid=41020&o_sch=Web +Property*

58 *Australia Census - FamilySearch.org - https://www.familysearch.org/wiki/en/Australia_Census*

59 *Researching your family - National Archives of Australia - http://www.naa.gov.au/collection/family-history/your-family/index.aspx*

If you know that one of your ancestors was in the military you could check out military documents through online genealogy websites.

Listed below are some websites to help in your ancestral search for military records available in your country:

- USA – Ancestry.com[60], Genealogy.com[61] (Article-Researching Through Military Records), MyHeritage[62], FindMyPast.com[63]

- UK – Ancestry.co.uk[64], The National Archives[65] (British Army soldiers after 1913), Forces War Records[66], FindMyPast.co.uk[67]

- Canada – Ancestry.ca[68], Library and Archives Canada[69], National Archives (Korean War)[70]

- Australia - Australian War Memorial[71], National Library of Australia[72], National Archives of Australia[73]

60 Military Records - Ancestry.com — https://search.ancestry.com/search/category.aspx?cat=39

61 Researching Through Military Records - Genealogy.com — http://www.genealogy.com/articles/research/00000106.html

62 Search Military Records - MyHeritage - https://www.myheritage.com/search-records

63 FindMyPast - https://www.findmypast.com/military-records/

64 Military Records - Ancestry.co.uk - https://search.ancestry.co.uk/search/category.aspx?cat=39

65 British Army soldiers after 1913 - The National Archives - http://www.nationalarchives.gov.uk/help-with-your-research/research-guides/british-army-soldiers-after-1913/

66 Forces War Records & Military Genealogy - https://www.forces-war-records.co.uk/

67 FindMyPast.co.uk - https://search.findmypast.co.uk/search-united-kingdom-records-in-military-armed-forces-and-conflict

68 Canadian Military Records – Ancestry.ca - https://search.ancestry.ca/search/group/ca_military

69 Military Heritage - Library and Archives Canada - http://www.bac-lac.gc.ca/eng/discover/military-heritage/Pages/military-heritage.aspx

70 Korean War Records - National Archives - https://www.archives.gov/research/military/korean-war

71 Personal Service Records: Australian Service - Australian War Memorial - https://www.awm.gov.au/research/guide/service-records

72 Where can I find Australian military records? - National Library of Australia - https://www.nla.gov.au/faq/where-can-i-find-australian-military-records

73 Service records - National Archives of Australia - http://www.naa.gov.au/collection/explore/defence/service-records/

Do you have ancestors who immigrated to the US, Canada or Australia? Were they pioneers who came over to the America's in search of adventure and a new life? Research ship passenger lists from various countries to get information you are seeking and watch your family tree saga grow. Below are some websites to help you in your quest:

- NewspaperARCHIVE.com[74]

- Ancestry.ca[75]

- Research to Find Canadian immigration records Library and Archives Canada[76]

- Olive Tree Genealogy[77]

- Ancestor Search[78]

74 *Newspaper Archives, Obituaries & Family History Records - NewspaperARCHIVE - NewspaperARCHIVE.com*

75 *Canadian immigration records - Ancestry.ca - http://www.ancestry.ca/cs/us/ca-immigration-records?kw1=&gclid=Cj0KCQiA2NXTBRDoARIsAJRIvLyLpcE54C-7orZbZSQZd4zQ0QkT0ZNUi_7-9IePaCthSXiCWvapoNcaAuYmEALw_wcB&s+kwcid=+canadian++passenger++lists&slid=&pgrid=20131369153&ptaid=aud-297763036715:kwd-32870200418&s_kwcid=+canadian++passenger++lists&kw2=Canadian+immigration+records&o_xid=59416&o_lid=59416&o_sch=Paid+Search+Non+Brand*

76 *Passenger Lists - Library and Archives Canada - https://www.bac-lac.gc.ca/eng/discover/immigration/immigration-records/passenger-lists/Pages/introduction.aspx*

77 *Ships Passenger Lists - Olive Tree Genealogy - https://www.olivetreegenealogy.com/ships/tocan1865-now.shtml*

78 *Passenger Lists to Canada - Ancestor Search - http://www.searchforancestors.com/locality/canada/passenger.html*

STEP 8

Find ancestors through city directories, land records court & prison records and in immigration & naturalization records

Getting to this step you probably have the genealogy bug and want to get as much detailed information and facts as you can.

Unearthing more facts about your ancestors is such a rush to find out how & where they lived. For example, if you are researching a grandfather from the 1800s in a city you know where they lived, you might be able to get the address or the plot of land where he lived and quite possibly his occupation.

If your ancestors did immigrate to the America's, you might be able to discover the dates, the ship they sailed on and the ports departed and where he arrived. All this information is great for your files and your Family Record Sheet.

Was there any so called 'bad apples' in your family? Did you have an ancestor who did prison time or have they been charged by the crown? You will be surprised what you will uncover and find when searching through prison and court records.

The details you discover slowly unweave a story of your family tree as more facts are revealed. Through hours of research you will have some good solid reliable information.

A story unfolds as you gather more information on the various families you are researching, you will definitely have something to share with your family in the future.

There are a number of different online search strategies for you to use such as searching city directories, land records, prison records, immigration and naturalization records.

You should now be familiar with researching your family tree and what websites that you may feel most comfortable with in your searches. Throughout this book, you have been given the tools and resources to complete your online research for your family tree in these areas. It is now up to you to be proactive and do it. I would suggest utilizing those resources with the information that have been provided throughout this book and the previous chapters to work further in your research.

Researching your ancestors will consume a lot of your time. Enjoy it while you can but don't forget your own family, spend time with them. They need you as much as you need them. Share your passion of the Family Tree and your genealogy with them and maybe you will have some assistants helping you in your family tree project.

Don't get lost and overwhelmed with everything in your search. Remember your goal and the priorities you have set in researching your family tree.

Below are some websites to help you in your search:

In Canada

City Directories - Canadian Directories Collection - Library and Archives Canada[79], CanGenealogy[80], Library and Archives Canada Blog[81]

Land Records - Library and Archives Canada - Land Records[82], Family Search Ontario Land and Property[83], Olive Tree Genealogy[84], Vancouver Public Library - Land Records[85]

Court & Prison Records - Court, Governmental & Criminal Records - Ancestry.ca[86], Prison & Convict Records in Canada - Black Sheep Ancestors[87], Canadian Criminal Records - Family History Alive[88]

Immigration & Naturalization Records - Ancestry.ca - Card Catalogue[89], Library and Archives Canada, Family Search[90]

---

79 *Canadian Directories Collection - Library and Archives Canada - https://www.bac-lac.gc.ca/eng/discover/directories-collection/Pages/directories-collection.aspx*

80 *CanGenealogy - http://www.cangenealogy.com/*

81 *Library and Archives Canada Blog - http://https://thediscoverblog.com/tag/city-directories/*

82 *Library and Archives Canada - Land Records - https://www.olivetreegenealogy.com/can/ont/land.shtml*

83 *Family Search Ontario Land and Property - https://www.familysearch.org/wiki/en/Ontario_Land_and_Property*

84 *Olive Tree Genealogy - Ontario Genealogy - Land Records - https://www.olivetreegenealogy.com/can/ont/land.shtml*

85 *Land records - Genealogy and Family History - Vancouver Public Library - - http://guides.vpl.ca/genealogy/landrecords*

86 *Court, Governmental & Criminal Records – Ancestry.ca — https://search.ancestry.ca/search/category.aspx?cat=141*

87 *Prison & Convict Records in Canada - Black Sheep Ancestors - http://www.blacksheepancestors.com/Canada/prisons.shtml*

88 *Canadian Criminal Records - Family History Alive - http://www.familyhistoryalive.com/Canadian-Criminal-Records.html*

89 *Ancestry.ca - Card Catalogue - https://search.ancestry.ca/search/CardCatalog.aspx#ccat=hc=25&dbSort=1&filter=0*40*

90 *Library and Archives Canada, Family Search - https://www.collectionscanada.gc.ca/whats-new/013-483-e.html*

In the US

City Directories – Ancestry.com[91], The Ancestor Hunt[92], Your Guide to Finding Ancestors in City Directories[93]

Land Records - Land Records – Ancestry.com[94], Family Search - US Land and Property[95], National Archives[96]

Court & Prison Records - Ancestry.com (Wills, Probates, Land, Tax & Criminal)[97], National Archives Court Records[98], Historical US Prison Records Online – ThoughtCo[99]

Immigration & Naturalization Records - Naturalization Records | National Archives[100], US Naturalization Records Indexes, 1794-1995 – Ancestry.com[101]

---

91 *US City Directories, 1822-1995 - Ancestry.com —* https://search.ancestry.com/search/db.aspx?dbid=2469

92 *Two Terrific Free Sites for Online City Directory Research (article) - The Ancestor Hunt -* http://www.theancestorhunt.com/blog/two-terrific-free-sites-for-online-citydirectoryresearch

93 *Your Guide to Finding Ancestors in City Directories - http://www.barbsnow.net/City Directories.html*

94 *Land Records – Ancestry.com — https://search.ancestry.ca/search/category.aspx? cat=144&geo_a=r&o_iid=41015&o_lid=41015&o_sch=Web+Property*

95 *Family Search - US Land and Property -* https://www.familysearch.org/wiki/en/United_States_Land_and_Property

96 *Land Records - National Archives - https://www.archives.gov/research/land*

97 *Wills, Probates, Land, Tax & Criminal – Ancestry.com —* https://search.ancestry.ca/search/category.aspx? cat=141&geo_a=r&o_iid=41015&o_lid=41015&o_sch=Web+Property

98 *Court Records - National Archives https://www.archives.gov/research/court-records*

99 *Historical US Prison Records Online – ThoughtCo -* https://www.thoughtco.com/historical-us-prison-records-online-1422333

100 *Naturalization Records | National Archives -* https://www.familysearch.org/wiki/en/United_States_Naturalization_and_Citizenship

101 *US Naturalization Records Indexes, 1794-1995 – Ancestry.com —* https://search.ancestry.com/search/db.aspx?dbid=1192

In UK

City Directories - Ancestry.co.uk[102], National Library of Scotland[103]

Land Records – Ancestry.co.uk[104], The National Archives[105]

Court & Prison Records - Prisoners and prison staff - The National Archives[106], Criminals and convicts - The National Archives[107], Prisoner / Trial / Conviction / Court Records UKGDL – Genealogical[108]

Immigration & Naturalization Records – Citizenship & Naturalisation Records – Ancestry.co.uk[109], Immigrants - The National Archives[110], Naturalization & Passport Records for England[111]

---

102 Ancestry.co.uk - https://search.ancestry.co.uk/search/db.aspx?dbid=1547

103 National Library of Scotland - https://www.nls.uk/family-history/directories

104 Ancestry.co.uk - https://search.ancestry.co.uk/search/category.aspx?cat=144

105 The National Archives - http://www.nationalarchives.gov.uk/help-with-your-research/research-guides/medieval-early-modern-family-history/

106 Prisoners and prison staff - The National Archives - http://www.nationalarchives.gov.uk/help-with-your-research/research-guides/prisoners-or-prison-staff/

107 Criminals and convicts - The National Archives - http://www.nationalarchives.gov.uk/help-with-your-research/research-guides/criminals-and-convicts/

108 Prisoner / Trial / Conviction / Court Records UKGDL – Genealogical - http://www.ukgdl.org.uk/category/prisoner_records

109 Citizenship & Naturalisation Records – Ancestry.co.uk - https://search.ancestry.co.uk/search/category.aspx?cat=115

110 Immigrants - The National Archives – http://www.nationalarchives.gov.uk/help-with-your-research/research-guides/immigrants/

111 Naturalization & Passport Records for England - http://www.naturalizationrecords.com/United_Kingdom.shtml

In Australia

City Directories - Australia Directories - Family Search[112], State Library Victoria - Researching your Victorian ancestors[113]

Land Records - Family Search - Australia Land and Property[114], State Library of Queensland[115], State Library Victoria - State & National Libraries[116]

Court & Prison Records - Australia Court Records Genealogy - FamilySearch Wiki[117], Court & police records - Court cases in Australia[118], Police gazettes, court and gaol records[119]

Immigration & Naturalization Records - Naturalization Index - State Archives and Records NSW[120], Migration and citizenship – National Archives of Australia[121], Immigration & Naturalisation - Researching your Victorian ancestors[122]

112 *Australia Directories - Family Search -*
   https://www.familysearch.org/wiki/en/Australia_Directories
113 *State Library Victoria - Researching your Victorian ancestors —*
   https://guides.slv.vic.gov.au/victorianancestors/directories
114 *Family Search - Australia Land and Property -*
   https://www.familysearch.org/wiki/en/Australia_Land_and_Property
115 *State Library of Queensland - http://www.slq.qld.gov.au/resources/family-history/land-
   records*
116 *State Library Victoria - State & National Libraries -*
   https://guides.slv.vic.gov.au/victorianancestors/directories
117 *Australia Court Records Genealogy - FamilySearch Wiki -*
   https://www.familysearch.org/wiki/en/Australia_Court_Records
118 *Court & police records - Court cases in Australia -*
   https://guides.slv.vic.gov.au/courtcases/courtandpolice
119 *Police gazettes, court and gaol records — http://aiatsis.gov.au/research/finding-your-
   family/family-history-sources/police-gazettes-court-and-gaol-records*
120 *Naturalization Index - State Archives and Records NSW -*
   *https://www.records.nsw.gov.au/archives/collections-and-research/guides-and-
   indexes/naturalization-index*
121 *Migration and citizenship – National Archives of Australia -*
   http://www.naa.gov.au/collection/explore/migration/index.aspx
122 *Immigration & Naturalisation - Researching your Victorian ancestors —*
   https://guides.slv.vic.gov.au/victorianancestors/immigration

STEP 9

Contact other relatives and descendants through ancestry website or Genealogy forum

This next step is to utilize the ancestry website or a Genealogy forum that you previously joined. Connect with potential ancestors to get more information on possible ancestors and distant cousins.

Search these websites and forums to connect with possible matches in your family tree. Compare ancestors on the websites with your tree and document where and with who you made contact with in your Contacts. Input whatever information you get into your Family Record Sheet.

Use the resources available to you to get as much information as you can on the people you are researching adding it to your documents.

In Chapter 5 the following steps will be covered:

Step 10 - Join a mailing list and search message boards through RootsWeb

Step 11 - Expand your family history resources and use social media (Facebook and Twitter) to make new connections

Step 12 - Read genealogy articles

Step 13 - Research online newspaper archives

CHAPTER FIVE

Steps 10 – 11 – 12 – 13

NETWORK YOUR FAMILY TREE AND LEARN

Genealogy... It's not the size of the tree that matters, it's the quality of the nuts you find on there!

In Chapter 4, the steps covered were 6, 7, 8 & 9. In those steps you learned how to research your ancestors through various online genealogy websites. Using those resources you got relevant information by locating birth and death records; using census records to obtain addresses and confirming family members; you searched military records for military service, you also researched ship's passenger lists and immigration records.

During this portion of your journey in researching family tree you should now expand your knowledge of genealogy by using the next four steps to gain access to more knowledge and skills learning from others.

The next four steps are:

Step 10 - Join a mailing list and search message boards through RootsWeb

Step 11 - Expand your family history resources and use social media (Facebook and Twitter) to make new connections

Step 12 - Read genealogy articles

Step 13 - Research online newspaper archives

Using these steps will give you information that is not already readily available on either Ancestry or Family Search.

STEP 10

Join a mailing list and search message boards through RootsWeb

RootsWeb[123] was first founded by genealogists and has been around the Internet for the past 30 years.

Why should you join RootsWeb?

Because it's "FREE"!

RootsWeb has the largest and most in-depth genealogical resources on the web. Join the site to gain access to the most unique user-contributed databases and you will be able to connect with the genealogy community from around the world. This invaluable genealogy information is not available anywhere else and is a priceless gem for family historians.

There are thousands of mailing lists and message boards for you so that you can research your family tree. It is a place for you and other fellow genealogists to share your research work and exchange information and ideas. Sharing and connecting with other people through a mailing list may connect you with distant relatives. This information will definitely help you in your family tree research.

An article in the Ancestry Magazine - Your Guide to RootsWeb[124] by Myra Vanderpool Gormley, CG which is available on Google Books, this is an excellent resource to read and to learn more about RootsWeb.

Become a member of a group through the many online mailing lists and message boards. Join and share to help you and others in the community in your ancestral research. Below are a few to help you in your quest:

---

123 *RootsWeb - https://wc.rootsweb.ancestry.com/*
124 *Ancestry Magazine - Your Guide to RootsWeb - https://books.google.ca/books id=IjgEAAAAMBAJ&pg=PA24&lpg=PA24&dq=why+use+Rootsweb&source=bl&ots=z 9hiNHdOYm&sig=nI4dIkDAHDZN2sJ0WGK_W81ygZ8&hl=en&sa=X&ved=0ahUKEwj Jgof6_JvZAhVh04MKHZ5kC24Q6AEIVzAI#v=onepage&q=why%20use %20Rootsweb&f=false*

Online mailing lists - Canada

- The Olive Tree Genealogy[125]
- Ontario Canada Mailing Lists - Canadian Genealogy[126]
- Ontario (Upper Canada) Genealogy and History Databases[127]
- Ontario GenWeb Project: Links - Geneofun.on.ca[128]

Online mailing lists - US

- Cyndi's List - Mailing Lists - Internet Resources[129]
- International Society of Genetic Genealogy Wiki[130]

Online mailing lists - UK

- Mailing Lists - Genuki[131]
- Register for UKGDL - Genealogical Directories and Lists Online for UK[132]

Online mailing lists - Australia

- Genealogy Links - Farmer Family[133]
- Cyndi's List - Australia - General Resources[134]

125 *The Olive Tree Genealogy - https://www.olivetreegenealogy.com/can/ont/ontmail.shtml*

126 *Ontario Canada Mailing Lists - Canadian Genealogy - http://www.canadiangenealogy.net/ontario/ontario_mailinglist.htm*

127 *Ontario (Upper Canada) Genealogy and History Databases - http://www.ontariogenealogy.com/database.html*

128 *Ontario GenWeb Project: Links – Geneofun.on.ca - http://www.geneofun.on.ca/db.php? database=ogwlinks&template=ogwlinks.html&search=TOPIC&sort=TITLE&max=200& find=misc*

129 *Cyndi's List - Mailing Lists - Internet Resources - https://www.cyndislist.com/mailing-lists/internet/*

130 *International Society of Genetic Genealogy Wiki - https://isogg.org/wiki/Genetic_genealogy_mailing_lists*

131 *Mailing Lists – Genuki - http://www.genuki.org.uk/indexes/MailingLists.html*

132 *Register for UKGDL - Genealogical Directories and Lists Online for UK - http://www.ukgdl.org.uk/register*

133 *Genealogy Links - Farmer Family - http://www.farmergroup.com/links.html*

134 *Cyndi's List - Australia - General Resources - https://www.cyndislist.com/australia/general/*

STEP 11

Expand your family history resources and use social media (Facebook and Twitter) to make new connections

"Making new connections"

Using social media and connecting with genealogy-focused feeds will provide you with valuable information. For example, Facebook is a great tool for genealogy to find distant relatives as you get in touch with family and to share photos. I would suggest you to use one service and then follow a couple more genealogy related feeds to expand your knowledge and share information.

Some online websites that you can use to follow genealogy blogs are on WordPress.com, Tumblr, GenealogyWise, LinkedIn, MySpace, Second Life, Google+, YouTube, Facebook, Twitter and Pinterest to name a few. Maybe you are already a member of some of these sites, all you need to do is join a few genealogy related sites and start networking.

Family Tree Magazine website is a great resource that has an excellent article with valuable information called the 'Social Media Mavericks: 40 to Follow'[135] by Lisa Louise Cooke.

Some social media links and resources to network your tree and yourself as you research are:

- A Guide to Using Social Media for Genealogy[136]

- Cyndi's List - Social Networking for Genealogy[137]

- Genealogical & Historical Groups/Pages on Facebook [138](in English) by Katherine R. Willson (pdf file)

---

135 *'Social Media Mavericks: 40 to Follow'* —
  https://www.familytreemagazine.com/premium/40-social-media-mavericks/

136 *A Guide to Using Social Media for Genealogy - https://blog.genealogybank.com/a-guide-to-using-social-media-for-genealogy.html*

137 *Cyndi's List - Social Networking for Genealogy - https://www.cyndislist.com/social-networking/*

138 *Genealogical & Historical Groups/Pages on Facebook (in English) By Katherine R. Willson - https://moonswings.files.wordpress.com/2017/11/genealogy-on-facebook-list-nov-20171.pdf*

- Facebook for Canadian Genealogy[139] by Gail Dever (pdf file)

- Australian History and Genealogy Groups and Pages on Facebook[140] by Alona Tester (pdf file)

- 10 Ways to Use Twitter for Genealogy[141] by Diane Haddad

---

139 Facebook for Canadian Genealogy - http://genealogyalacarte.ca/wp-content/uploads/2018/02/Facebook-for-Canadian-Genealogy-February-2018.pdf

140 Australian History and Genealogy Groups and Pages on Facebook http://www.lonetester.com/wp-content/uploads/2016/09/Facebook-Genealogy-Australia-2016-09-10.pdf

141 10 Ways to Use Twitter for Genealogy by Diane Haddad - https://www.familytreemagazine.com/articles/genealogy-fun/social-networking/10-ways-to-use-twitter-for-genealogy/

STEP 12

Read genealogy articles

Genealogy articles is a valuable resource when you research as it is a great way to unearth information from the past. You just have to know where to look and get this information. For any genealogist, finding documentation of your ancestors all depends on what information that you are looking for in your search.

One of the main reasons to read genealogy articles is to learn and expand your knowledge. Reading an article may uncover an ancestor you are researching thus learning more details about their life and where you came from. You can learn a lot through these articles as they are well worth the reading. Reading articles will definitely provide you with more genealogy knowledge and tools.

There are thousands of websites with genealogy articles and every one of them will have something of value for you. The information that you read during your research is like researching your family tree.

Which website provides truthful documentation?

Does the website have reliable sources?

You should be a little skeptical in the information that each website provides. As a genealogist, you should check on the author's credentials for accuracy, are they reputable, do they provide good resources within the genealogy community.

Below are some websites with links to plenty of genealogy articles to get you started. I hope you find some of these resources interesting and useful in your family tree research.

- Genealogy In Time[142]
- High-Definition Genealogy[143]
- Family History Daily[144]
- Olive Tree Genealogy[145]
- Genealogy.com[146]

---

142 *Genealogy In Time - http://www.genealogyintime.com/genealogy-articles.html*

143 *High-Definition Genealogy - https://hidefgen.com/articles/*

144 *Family History Daily - https://familyhistorydaily.com/category/free-genealogy-resources/*

145 *Olive Tree Genealogy – Articles - https://www.olivetreegenealogy.com/articles/*

146 *Genealogy.com - http://www.genealogy.com*

STEP 13

Research online newspaper archives

Using online newspapers is a good family tree resource tool in getting information. If you were researching through old newspapers and you found out that one of your great grandfather's had immigrated to the America's in the early 1700s, that would be an awesome find.

In the newspaper article it divulged the information of the ship's name, date and time of arrival, and the passengers onboard the ship. In the paper you come across his name and the people he travelled with. You would then have another piece of the puzzle to your family tree with a good source of information. Make the necessary citation reference in your journal or record sheet. BRAVO! You can cross-reference this information with other the documentation and evidence you already have on him.

Information from old newspapers will provide some of these details when you do a search:

- birth announcements
- marriage announcements
- divorces
- obituaries or death notices
- name changes
- employment
- addresses
- military records
- significant events such as family reunions
- daily life events
- court documents and cases
- immigration and ships' passenger lists

Below is a list of newspaper websites to start your search:

- The Ancestor Hunt[147] - Lists newspapers searches for the US, Canada, World

- Cyndi's List - Canada - Newspapers[148]

- Library of Congress - Chronicling America[149]

- Illinois Digital Newspaper Collection[150]

- GenealogyBank - Historical Newspapers[151]

- Google News Archive[152]

- Library and Archives Canada - Newspaper Collection[153]

- Canada, Newspaper Archive[154]

- BRITISH Newspaper Archives 1607-2013 NewspaperArchive®[155]

- British Newspaper Archive[156]

- Trove - National Library of Australia[157]

- Australia Newspaper Archives (1840-1979)[158]

---

147 *The Ancestor Hunt - http://www.theancestorhunt.com/newspaper-research-links.html#.WoYvIhclHys*

148 *Cyndi's List - Canada » Newspapers - https://www.cyndislist.com/canada/newspapers/*

149 *Library of Congress - Chronicling America - https://chroniclingamerica.loc.gov/search/titles/*

150 *Illinois Digital Newspaper Collection - http://idnc.library.illinois.edu/*

151 *GenealogyBank - Historical Newspapers - https://www.genealogybank.com/explore/newspapers/all*

152 *Google News Archive - https://news.google.com/newspapers?hl=en*

153 *Library and Archives Canada - Newspaper Collection - https://www.bac-lac.gc.ca/eng/discover/newspapers/newspaper-collection/Pages/canadian-news-online.aspx*

154 *Canada, Newspaper Archive - https://newspaperarchive.com/ca/*

155 *BRITISH Newspaper Archives 1607-2013 NewspaperArchive® - https://newspaperarchive.com/uk/*

156 *British Newspaper Archive - https://www.britishnewspaperarchive.co.uk/*

157 *Trove - National Library of Australia - https://trove.nla.gov.au/newspaper/*

158 *Australia Newspaper Archives (1840-1979) — https://newspaperarchive.com/au/*

In Chapter 6 the following four steps will be covered:

Step 14 - Check websites that offer historical or genealogical societies in the area you're researching

Step 15 - Subscribe to a free newsletter or a blog

Step 16 - Check out funeral home records

Step 17 - Check out online cemetery records and visit them, record and take photographs of your findings

Additional websites to expand your search, I would recommend reading some of these excellent articles as they also have plenty of free ancestry research sources to help you along:

- Top Databases for Canadian Genealogy Research[159]

- Ancestry for Free: Genealogy Research Sites That Don't Cost a Dime[160]

- How to View Thousands of Free Records on Ancestry Without a Subscription[161]

- Free ancestry resources on FindMyPast[162]

- Treasure Maps Genealogy[163]

- Family Tree - Canada Genealogy[164]

- Family Tree - Ontario Online Genealogy Records[165]

---

159 *Top Databases for Canadian Genealogy Research -*
https://www.thoughtco.com/databases-and-websites-for-canadian-genealogy-1421730
160 *Ancestry for Free: Genealogy Research Sites That Don't Cost a Dime*
https://familyhistorydaily.com/family-history/ancestry-for-free-family-history-research-without-spending-a-cent/
161 *How to View Thousands of Free Records on Ancestry Without a Subscription*
https://familyhistorydaily.com/genealogy-resources/ancestry-com-offers-600-free-searchable-collections/
162 *Free ancestry resources on FindMyPast - https://www.findmypast.co.uk/free-ancestry-records*
163 *Treasure Maps Genealogy - http://amberskyline.com/treasuremaps/*
164 *Family Tree - Canada Genealogy -*
https://www.familysearch.org/wiki/en/Canada_Genealogy
165 *Family Tree - Ontario Online Genealogy Records -*
https://www.familysearch.org/wiki/en/Ontario_Online_Genealogy_Records

NOTES

CHAPTER SIX

Steps 14 – 15 – 16 – 17

GENEALOGICAL KNOWLEDGE

Genealogy: Chasing your own tale!

Researching your family genealogy for documented facts and evidence is a continuing process. You will continue your search on ancestors and the most important thing I can't stress enough is to document it.

Last chapter we covered Steps 10, 11, 12 & 13.

During those steps you learned about online tools by joining and accessing mailing lists and searching message boards through RootsWeb. You expanded your family history resources using social media websites, becoming more knowledgeable reading genealogy articles and researching online newspaper archives.

Genealogy research seemed endless when you first start but the main goal is putting together an awesome family tree for future generations. The learning curve for genealogy might have seemed an unreachable goal at the beginning but as you expand your knowledge you gain more skillsets and develop a genealogy background to help others who are also learning.

Genealogy is like a puzzle as you unweave your ancestors lives into a beautiful scenic picture with a large tree on the horizon. New life begins as branches extend out from the trunk into new leaves. Those new leaves are yours' and your distant cousins' children and grandchildren. The cycle will repeat itself over and over again.

Stay focused, the hours of research will positively multiply uncovering a history filled family saga of your ancestors.

The more tools you have to access your roots will make researching you family tree highly rewarding. The results will fill you with pride for what you have accomplished.Continuing on this journey, the next four steps are:

Step 14 - Check websites that offer historical or genealogical societies in the area you're researching

Step 15 - Subscribe to a free newsletter or a blog

Step 16 - Check out funeral home records

Step 17 - Check out online cemetery records and visit them, record and take photographs of your findings

STEP 14

Check websites that offer historical or genealogical societies in the area that you are researching

There are plenty of benefits for joining and being a member of a 'Local Family History Society or Group'. One advantage is that it will help you extend your family tree with connections to the local history, people, and the records in the area. It will increase your knowledge and research skills. Many societies publish helpful journals, transcripts, and they also have compiled genealogies.

Being a member of a genealogical society is one of the best ways in finding and connecting with other relatives and to compare family trees. It is also a great way to learn about the events and the local history that affected your ancestors during their lives.

As a member it allows you to interact with fellow members through forums, mailing lists, email and even instant messaging. Sharing and collaborating with others with local knowledge will help you in connecting with the local archives and libraries.

If you are at a standstill in your search a genealogical society may help you in overcoming these brick-walls and continue your genealogy search with more effective search strategies. Becoming a member of a society will open new doors in your search.

If you are interested in a town or village in a part of the county where your ancestor lived, I would just type in your query in the search bar of your browser and then go from there. Get some preliminary information of the local area first.

A good URL and a place to start would be the Wikipedia - List of historical societies[166], this is a dynamic and partial list for around the world.Since I am from Ontario, Canada I would start with these website resources to begin my search:

- The Ontario Genealogical Society[167]

- CanGenealogy[168]

- Cyndi's List - Canada - Provinces - Ontario - Societies & Groups[169]

Using these links will definitely keep you busy researching for months or even years. Join and become a member of a couple of them to get your feet wet. Any way you look at it, it is a highly valuable resource to network yourself and your family tree.

If you are from another province or country you will probably find other websites tailored for your search.

166 Wikipedia - List of historical societies
    https://en.wikipedia.org/wiki/List_of_historical_societies
167 The Ontario Genealogical Society - https://ogs.on.ca/
168 CanGenealogy - http://www.cangenealogy.com/
169 Cyndi's List - Canada - Provinces - Ontario - Societies & Groups -
    https://www.cyndislist.com/canada/provinces/on/societies/

STEP 15

Subscribe to a free newsletter or a blog

Subscribe, read, learn and enlighten your ancestral knowledge. Hone your genealogy detective skills by subscribing and reading newsletters or a blog from different genealogy websites. It will definitely give you inspiration in your searches.

Once you subscribe to a newsletter it is sent out weekly or monthly. It is sent by the author's website through it's email system to other genealogy enthusiasts and researchers providing free genealogy research help, tips, news and updates.

A blog is an online journal that is very similar to a newspaper or magazine and is usually updated daily. The blog can then be read online on the website or it can be set up on a browser-based feed reader, known as a RSS feed.

You can subscribe to as many genealogy blog feeds and then read them whenever you want to.

Some websites for you to check out:

- Internet Genealogy[170]

- Genealogy Newsletter[171]

- Cyndi's List - Magazines[172]

- Family History Daily[173]

- Ancestry Magazine - Google Books[174] - Ancestry magazine issues from 1994-2010

- Family Search Blog[175]

---

170 *Internet Genealogy - https://internet-genealogy.com/*

171 *Genealogy Newsletter - http://www.genealogynewsletter.com/*

172 *Cyndi's List – Magazines - https://www.cyndislist.com/magazines/e-zines/*

173 *Family History Daily - https://familyhistorydaily.com/genealogy-resources/50-free-genealogy-sites/*

174 *Ancestry Magazine - Google Books - https://books.google.ca/books?id=Yg4iWBma2eQC&source=gbs_all_issues_r&cad=1&atm_aiy=1990#all_issues_anch or*

175 *Family Search Blog - https://www.familysearch.org/blog/en/*

STEP 16

Check out funeral home records

Researching funeral home records at funeral homes or online allows you to find information and details that is not usually on the death certificate. Some information that you may get is a list of names and addresses of surviving relatives, a copy of the obituary, funeral arrangements, parents names, place of birth, etc.

The information you get accessing the funeral home records will be very useful in your family tree research. Below are some links to start:

- Funeral Home Records Genealogy - FamilySearch Wiki[176]

- How to Find Funeral Home Records - About Genealogy - ThoughtCo[177]

- US, Cemetery and Funeral Home Collection, 1847-2018 - Ancestry.com[178]

- Funeral Home Records - Ancestors At Rest[179]

176 *Funeral Home Records Genealogy - FamilySearch Wiki -*
   https://www.familysearch.org/wiki/en/Funeral_Home_Records
177 *How to Find Funeral Home Records - About Genealogy – ThoughtCo -*
   https://www.thoughtco.com/family-history-in-funeral-home-records-1421815
178 *US, Cemetery and Funeral Home Collection, 1847-2018*
   https://search.ancestry.com/search/db.aspx?dbid=2190
179 *Funeral Home Records - Ancestors At Rest http://ancestorsatrest.com/funeral_recs/*

STEP 17

Check out online cemetery records and visit them, record and take photographs of your findings

As a genealogist you need to see original records from a single source and what better place to get that information than searching online cemetery records. Once you get that information — record what you find into a family tree journal or your Family Group Record Sheet.

To help you in your search you could use FindAGrave.com[180] or billiongraves.com[181] websites to get information. Whichever website that you use, all you have to do is open your favorite browser, search for a specific cemetery and start your search.

Depending on the information and detail of your search, the online cemetery may have a very significant source of historical information on your ancestor. Every bit of info you find is verification of your family member.

At the FindAGrave website, info you will get will be:

- Birth Date (if known)

- Death Date

- Burial Place

- Memorial ID Number

Other information may be displayed on the webpage such as a headstone photo, additional photos, a list of other family members and possibly a unique story of the person.

You might want to check out Interment.net - Cemetery Records Online[182], you can browse by country, state or province, city, cemetery and then enter in your ancestor's name. The website is powered by GenealogyBank[183]. It is a clean looking website and very quick. The website scans records of the

---

180 *Find A Grave - http://Findagrave.com/*

181 *billiongraves.com - http://billiongraves.com/*

182 *Interment.net - Cemetery Records Online - http://www.interment.net/Default.htm*

183 *GenealogyBank - https://www.genealogybank.com/static/lp/internment/?*
   intver=1501IntroDefault&pq=1&prebuy=yes&utm_campaign=1204IT30lp&utm_source
   =1204IT30lp&utm_medium=1204IT30lp&s_siteloc=1204IT30lp&s_trackval=1204IT30l
   p&s_referrer=1204IT30lp&kbid=69919&CCPRODCODE=1204IT

cemeteries where your ancestors are buried. You will be extremely pleased wth the documentation and reference.

On the Interment website, the cemetery where my paternal grandmother is buried, the record displayed this detailed result:

"Gibbs, Reta Isabella (Cross), female, b. July 23, 1912, Norwood, ON, d. July 11, 2008, Ptbo Regional Health Centre, bur. July 15, 2008, age: 95, Location: R17L24#3 n.w., next of kin: Alice Chambers, daughter"

Note: I was very pleased with the report. There was a lot of information in it and it all depends on whoever transcribes the information into the cemetery's logbook. Some cemetery's may not have as much information or they may have more.

Going to the cemetery (office) and to the gravesite where your ancestor is buried is a very important thing for any genealogist to do, even if it is to only pay your respects. The existing cemetery records also known as the sexton's records include burial registers, plat maps and plot records. A sexton is the cemetery's caretaker, they may be able to help you in your search leading you to other relatives.

While you are at your ancestor's gravesite, record your findings and be as accurate as possible. Write down exactly what is on the headstone such as names, dates, spouse's name, inscriptions and sketch any symbols. The information on the inscription will provide valuable genealogical information. Take photographs or even better, videotape all sides of the headstone. The headstone can provide important information and is excellent source documentation for your records.

You just never know what genealogy gem you will find in the cemetery. Nearby gravestones might lead you to other members of the family or distant relatives as relatives were normally and possibly buried close to one another.

An excellent article on Cemetery Research[184] by Dae Powell it is an informative guide to use when you go to do any cemetery research, you may have other ways to do it yourself but if you're a new genealogist I would suggest using these steps. This guide will help you immensely as a genealogist and you can change or modify the method to suit your needs.

There are plenty of websites available online for you to conduct a cemetery search. So whatever country that your ancestor died, I would initiate a search there first and input as much information on the website as you can. Start with your country first and then the cemetery following up with a visit

---

184 Cemetery Research – Shoestring Genealogy – Article
   http://www.shoestringgenealogy.com/article/Cemetery.htm

to the parish church or cemetery to do your fact finding.

To help you with your online cemetery record search check out these links:

- Vital Records | National Archives US[185]
- Family Search - United States Death Records[186]
- Burial Records & Death Records in the UK[187]
- Cyndi's List Death Records[188]
- Ancestor Search[189]
- Ontario Cemetery Finding Aid[190]
- Online Death Indexes and Records for Canada[191]
- Find A Grave[192]
- Canadian Headstone Photo Project[193]
- Interment.net[194]

In the next Chapter, the final five steps from 18 – 22 will be covered:

Step 18 - Go to locations where your ancestors came from

Step 19 - Re-evaluate your research and ensure everything is well documented with reference citations

Step 20 - Create your own Family Tree Record Sheets and Pedigree Charts

Step 21 - Backup your personal or online files onto a USB flash drive and properly label it

Step 22 - Share and publish your family tree

---

185 *Vital Records | National Archives US - https://www.archives.gov/research/vital-records*

186 *Family Search - United States Death Records - https://www.familysearch.org/wiki/en/United_States_Death_Records*

187 *Burial Records & Death Records in the UK - https://www.ukburials.com*

188 *Cyndi's List Death Records - https://www.cyndislist.com/death/*

189 *Ancestor Search - http://www.searchforancestors.com/locality/canada/cemetery.html*

190 *Ontario Cemetery Finding Aid - http://ocfa.islandnet.com/homepage.html*

191 *Online Death Indexes and Records for Canada - https://www.deathindexes.com/canada.html*

192 *Find a Grave - https://www.findagrave.com/*

193 *Canadian Headstone Photo Project - https://canadianheadstones.com/*

194 *Interment.net - http://Interment.net/*

NOTES

CHAPTER SEVEN

Steps 18 – 19 – 20 – 21 – 22

ONSITE ANCESTRAL RESEARCH

"To forget one's ancestor is to be a brook without a source, a tree without a root." - Chinese proverb

Congratulations for getting to the last phase in the steps that I think are required in researching your family tree. This is the last chapter for the "22 STEPS in RESEARCHING YOUR FAMILY TREE".

The first 17 steps listed below were all covered in the previous chapters.

1. Start with yourself
2. Gather what information you already have or know
3. Start the search with one family at a time by talking to family members and relatives
4. Become a member of an online ancestry website
5. Join an online Genealogy forum
6. Obtain or locate copies of birth certificates or baptism records, marriage records, death or burial records and obituary notices
7. Find ancestors in Census Records, Military documents and ship's passenger lists
8. Find ancestors through city directories, land records court & prison records and in immigration & naturalization records
9. Contact other relatives and descendants through ancestry website or Genealogy forum
10. Join a mailing list and search message boards through RootWeb
11. Expand your family history resources and use social media (Facebook and Twitter) to make new connections
12. Read genealogy articles
13. Research online newspaper archives
14. Check websites that offer historical or genealogical societies in the area that you're researching
15. Subscribe to a free newsletter or a blog
16. Check out funeral home records

17. Check out online cemetery records and visit them, record and take photographs of your findings

You have come a long way through these 17 Steps and I am sure you have researched extensively while enlarging your family tree discovering new ancestors. It is quite a thrill learning about yourself and where you came from.

Get ready to do some onsite research!

Now is the time to complete the final five steps in effectively researching your family tree:

Step 18 - Go to locations where your ancestors came from

Step 19 - Re-evaluate your research and ensure everything is well documented with reference citations

Step 20 - Create your own Family Tree Record Sheets and Pedigree Charts

Step 21 - Backup your personal or online files onto a USB flash drive and properly label it

Step 22 - Share and publish your family tree

STEP 18

Go to locations where your ancestors came from

As you conduct research on your family tree where your ancestors lived, it would be a great idea to visit those locations.

First, research the location online, take notes and get information on the area before you do take the trip. Completing this step will open up your visual senses as you imagine what it was like to live when and where your relative was alive.

Put on your hiking shoes or boots and do some backwoods research and envision walking where your ancestors lived in a previous time and past.

Take pictures or record a video of the area for your records of the churches, cemeteries, schools, city or town hall. Visit the library researching old maps and explore the local history section. You just might uncover something unique about your family.

Visiting these locations will give you meaningful connections of your family history and ancestors. Whatever you uncover will be excellent data for your research. Ensure that you take photos of older buildings as some of these structures will give you an idea of what it looked like at the time.

Talk to the local residents. The information you gather will substantiate your findings and the records you have already. Overall whatever you reveal in your findings it will give you a sense of identity and cultural heritage.

STEP 19

Re-evaluate your research and ensure everything is well documented with reference citations

Researching your family tree is a project that all genealogists realize that has no end. It is a continuous and ongoing process.

Re-evaluate your research by going through your records ensuring that the documents are reliable, the source material matches your search correctly and you have accurate citations.

Re-adjust your findings with any new references and add them to your records. Repeating this step on your family tree will occasionally reveal new evidence and more information giving you a real sense of accomplishment.

STEP 20

Create your own Family Tree Record Sheets and Pedigree Charts

In Chapter 2, I talked about Family Record Sheets and Pedigree Charts with download links for these forms so that you can document your family tree information. Record your information in a neat and orderly method.

If you haven't done so, now would be a good time as your documents will increase to grow.

Download or create a Family Record Sheet and a Pedigree Chart on each family you are researching. Complete each form with the data you have collected attaching any documents and photographs to the family record.

You can either save and record these files in organized folders on your computer or keep hard copies of them in binders or journals.

If you joined an online genealogy website, save any additional information you get on the online file. The more data you save online the more detail each individual file will have for your records. Once your tree starts to take shape and grow you will be able to download the GEDCOM file and add it to a Free Standalone Genealogy Program (ie. Family Tree Maker).

Research online genealogy websites, read the descriptions of each and then compare programs:

- Best Genealogy Software of 2018[195]

- Best Free Online Genealogy or Family Tree Application[196]

- Best Free Genealogy or Family Tree Software[197]

---

195 *Best Genealogy Software of 2018 - http://www.toptenreviews.com/software/home/best-genealogy-software/*

196 *Best Free Online Genealogy or Family Tree Applications - https://www.techsupportalert.com/content/best-free-online-genealogy-family-tree-applications.htm*

197 *Best Free Genealogy or Family Tree Software - https://www.techsupportalert.com/best-free-genealogy-family-tree-software.htm*

STEP 21

Backup your personal or online files onto a USB flash drive and properly label it

As you collect documents on your family tree it is imperative that you need to start backing up all your personal or online files.

Store miscellaneous documents such as personal stories, newspaper articles, birth, baptismal, marriage and death certificates, they are all important facts and special. They need to be stored properly.

Any old photographs that you have collected during your search need to be saved. It is very important to digitize, label and store them all into a safe place. Photoshop Express Editor[198] is a free online photo editor where you can be creative. You will be able to professionally preserve or enhance and improve the quality of your photographs. Once you have all your photos grouped by individual family units, save them into a separate folder on your computer then back them up.

A good source of information to use is available on the FamilySearch[199] website, use the suggestions as a reference to preserve and store your treasured keepsakes. The information on the website has a lot of tips and tools. There is a valuable set of guidelines on storing all your documents and photographs, properly and safely.

Expect the unexpected in case of a disaster, back up your files. Its better to be safe than sorry. Make sure that you save all your documents and files onto either CD's/DVD's or a USB Flash Drive (recommended).

Use a free online data website as an extra source of storage and security. There are a number of free ones available on the Internet and I would definitely use one.

---

198 *Photoshop Express Editor - https://www.photoshop.com/tools?wf=editor*
199 *FamilySearch – Preserving Photographs & Documents*
  https://www.familysearch.org/wiki/en/Preserving_Photographs_&_Documents

Here is a short list of the best free online data websites with maximum storage space for your files:

- Google Drive[200] – provides 15 GB of space for new users
- pCloud[201] – 10 GB (expandable)
- Microsoft OneDrive[202] – 5 GB
- MediaFire[203] - 10 GB (expandable)

You can also buy extra storage space on these websites if you need the extra space.

An excellent article about Free Online Storage on the website MoneySavingExpert[204] to read that has great information keeping your online storage secure.

---

200 Google Drive - https://www.google.com/drive/

201 pCloud - https://www.pcloud.com

202 Microsoft OneDrive – http://www.onedrive.live.com/

203 MediaFire - https://www.mediafire.com

204 Money Saving Expert - https://www.moneysavingexpert.com/shopping/free-online-storage

STEP 22

Share and publish your family tree

Ah, the last step!

Remember the process does repeats itself and is never ending.

During this step it is important for you to share everything you have gathered on your family tree in an awe inspiring and creative manner. Sharing your tree with others is another way in finding other ancestors and distant cousins.

How will I share my family tree?

Well, there are a number of ways to share your family tree, below are some suggestions:

With family and friends

- Connecting and sharing with family will lead you to more information that you probably don't already have opening up new paths and discoveries for your journey into the past.

- Share with a friend who is like minded in genealogy. You will be able to share ideas and brain storm thoughts if you hit a brick-wall. It could lead you down a different unexplored road and make it all worthwhile in your search.

- Share on paid ancestry websites such as Ancestry.com[205], FamilySearch[206] or MyHeritage[207]; sharing on free websites such as WikiTree[208] or WeRelate[209].

- Add your GEDCOM[210] family tree file and connect with other genealogists researching the same name search. Searching same

---

205 *Ancestry - https://search.ancestry.com/search/db.aspx?dbid=1030*

206 *FamilySearch - https://www.familysearch.org/wiki/en/Main_Page*

207 *MyHeritage - http://www.myheritage.com/*

208 *WikiTree - https://www.wikitree.com/*

209 *WeRelate - https://www.werelate.org/wiki/Main_Page*

210 *GEDCOM is short for GEnealogical Data COMmunication. Originally developed in 1985, a GEDCOM file is the most common method of formatting your family tree data into a text file to exchange genealogical information. The GEDCOM is easily read and converted by any genealogy software program. https://www.thoughtco.com/genealogy-gedcom-basics-1421891*

family names will lead you to discover new cousins or distant ancestors you never knew about, uncovering a new gem for your treasure chest.

- Share on social media websites on the genealogy pages such as Facebook[211] and Twitter[212].

Someone you know on a social media website knows a person that you might be related to. You are introduced and realize the person is a third cousin four times removed because you both have a common ancestor.

Networking and sharing your genealogy ideas on a social media website increases your knowledge.

Internet genealogy message boards

- Leave some family tree information for others, they may be searching someone in your tree and vice versa.

- An excellent tool to leave specific questions and get answers to family tree queries.

- There are knowledgeable genealogists online who are more than willing to help others, all you have to do is ask. Sharing is the key to a well documented family saga.

Self Publish your own genealogy web page

- Start a genealogy website that generates traffic that is accessible worldwide.

- Share your tree so that your family has access to the information that you already have.

- Family and friends can leave feedback on the website; and either email or call you.

- Family information for your descendants

Self Publish a genealogy e-book or paperback

- Once you think you have enough data and documents on your family tree, share your tree creating a family e-book.

- Create a visual family tree document to be passed down from generation to generation. A family heirloom left to your great-great grandson's or daughter's of their genealogy. A well-documented e-book or paperback they can be proud of displaying on their coffee

---

211 Facebook - *https://www.facebook.com/*
212 Twitter - *https://twitter.com/login?lang=en*

tables.

- Self-publish your family tree e-book into a photo book.

- Hire a publisher-for-hire to help you publish a professional document if you don't have the skills for creating the project.

- Create a Print-On-Demand version of your e-book so relatives can purchase a copy.

Below are a few good references to research and read to motivate you in sharing and self publishing your story:

- How to Self-Publish Your Family History Book[213]

- How to Prepare Your Family History Manuscript for Publication[214]

- Writing and Publishing Your Family History[215]

- Join and participate in a family or surname association

- Create a genealogy network with your surname.

- Other fellow genealogists on these websites may be researching the same surname as you. This alone could lead you to more contacts on your family tree.

213 *How to Self-Publish Your Family History Book -*
  https://www.familytreemagazine.com/premium/publishing-your-family-history/
214 *How to Prepare Your Family History Manuscript for Publication -*
  https://www.thoughtco.com/publishing-your-family-history-book-1422316
215 *Writing and Publishing Your Family History -*
  https://www.americanancestors.org/education/learning-resources/read/writing-publishing

LESSONS LEARNED

Everyone that takes genealogy seriously may do it differently but these steps are all essential for you to achieve your goal in researching your family tree.

By this stage you should have now gained enough genealogy knowledge and tools to confidently research your family roots. Using this help guide will definitely assist you in becoming a better family historian.

Genealogy never ends, the process repeats itself and the cycle continues from generation to generation until the end of time.

I hope that you have found the '22 Steps In Researching Your Family Tree' useful while you researched your family tree. Please share your genealogy knowledge with others.

Listen, research, read, learn,

document, participate, ask questions and share.

CHAPTER EIGHT

Addendum

GENEALOGY DNA TESTING

Do you know who you are and where you came from?

If not, then a DNA test is in order.

As you are well aware, DNA Testing is available for family genealogists to discover more about themselves. There is a number of advertisements in magazines, on the television and widely on the Internet today giving more people the opportunity to find out more about themselves in detail.

Today there is so much to learn about your family tree. Having the opportunity to get your DNA tested is a positive way in discovering who we are and where we came from. Do your own research on DNA testing and discover more about yourself and your ancestors.

Getting your DNA tested for genealogy purposes will inform you where your ancestors came from. You will then be able to hone into various areas where your ancestors gene pool is heavily populated finding distant cousins and living relatives.

Imagine the thrill of getting DNA matches from other possible relatives from around the globe to further your Family Tree research.

There are three types of DNA testing that you can get done but for most genealogists, the autosomal DNA test would be the one to have analyzed and tested.

The three types of DNA testing available are:

- Autosomal DNA Test - determines how closely related you are to someone else and is ideal to go back as far as 4 or 5 generations. Possibly find living relatives who are searching the same families as you are. This testing can be used for estimating of your ethnicity, or the regions of the world where your ancestors lived.

- mtDNA or Mitochondrial DNA Test - can be costly and is good for discovering a common ancestor. Testing is done on your maternal line only and is passed down exclusively from your mother. The ancestry results are very precise and accurate while it only helps you trace one line.

- Y-DNA Tests - this test can only tell you about your direct paternal line. The test would be ideal for anyone who was adopted to discover the paternal side of his or her family and is useful if you want to prove a connection to a certain ancestor.

A good article called the Best DNA Test for Ancestry[216] can be read in more detail at Smarterhobby.com. There is a list of five Ancestry DNA websites that have been tested whereby you can view a comparison chart for information purposes while you research.

The five Ancestry DNA websites compared and tested with links so you can decide which one would be best suited for you:

- AncestryDNA[217] - A autosomal DNA test is collected, saliva sample is used and analyzed to examine clues about your family history. Current price is for $99 US.

- FamilyTreeDNA[218] - Provides separate testing for all types available by a cheek swab sample. Regular pricing from $79 to $199 US

- MyHeritage DNA[219] - A simple autosomal cheek swab DNA test is used and analyzed to discover your ethnic origins and sells for $99 US

- 23andMe[220] - Provides two testing options which is submitted in a saliva collection kit to the lab for analysis, the Ancestry Service for $99 US, and the Health + Ancestry Service for $199 US

- Living DNA[221] - This is the 3-in-1 Ancestry Test provides testing results for of all three types available. Regular price is $99 US

Discover more about yourself! Take your family tree research to the next level and get your DNA tested. Get educated with as much info as you can and research the DNA testing that is available today.

An article to read to help you in deciding which one would be good for you can be read at Top 10 DNA Testing[222] which was updated in August 2018.

In my opinion it is a toss up between AncestryDNA and MyHeritageDNA. It is all up to you which one would be best in your personal preferences. I would be more inclined to go with Ancestry DNA testing since my family tree is already on the website and I would have more options in my research later.

---

216 *Best DNA Test for Ancestry - https://www.smarterhobby.com/genealogy/best-dna-test/*
217 *AncestryDNA - www.ancestry.ca/dna/*
218 *FamilyTreeDNA - www.familytreedna.com/*
219 *MyHeritage DNA - www.myheritage.com/dna*
220 *23andMe DNA - www.23andme.com/en-ca*
221 *Living DNA - www.livingdna.com/*
222 *Top 10 DNA Testing (Aug 2018) - www.top10bestdnatesting.com/*

Get your DNA testing done to boldly go where you want to uncover more about your roots!

I hope that this chapter helps you in your family tree research to discover more about yourself and finding more relatives in your gene pool from your ancestors.

Good luck in all your ancestral discoveries!

NOTES

RECOMMENDED SHORT READING LIST

Helen Osborn, Genealogy: Essential Research Methods, (Dec 1 2012)

George G. Morgan and Drew Smith, Advanced Genealogy Research Techniques, (First Edition Sep 10 2013)

George G. Morgan, How to Do Everything: Genealogy, (Fourth Edition Feb 2 2015)

Marsha Hoffman Rising, The Family Tree Problem Solver: Tried and True Tactics for Tracing Elusive   Ancestors, (First Edition Apr 19 2011)

Drew Smith, Organize Your Genealogy: Strategies and Solutions for Every Researcher, (Jul 1 2016)

Blaine T. Bettinger, The Family Tree Guide to DNA Testing and Genetic Genealogy, (Oct 13 2016)

Thomas MacEntee, 500 Best Genealogy & Family History Tips 2015 Edition, (Nov 25 2014)

Amy Johnson Crow, 31 Days to Better Genealogy (Kindle Edition 1.0), (May 2017)

RECOMMENDED DOWNLOAD LIST

- A downloadable OneNote Family Tree file called 'Surname Notebook – Sources sorted in Chronological Order[223]' from Erin Williamson Klein

- Available from The Family Historian website 'Free Fillable Genealogy Forms[224]'

- Free Genealogy Forms and Charts[225] from genealogysearcg.org

- Various downloadable Charts and Forms from Ancestry.com[226]

The information and link below is for some recommended eBooks from Ancestral Findings.com, there are 11 ebooks available to download. All you have to do is subscribe to the website.

- Free Ancestral eBooks[227]

223 *Surname Notebook – Sources sorted in Chronological Order -* *http://myfamilyhistoryfiles.com/onenote-a-to-z/*

224 *Free Fillable Genealogy Forms - http://thefamilyhistorian.com.au/free-downloads/genealogy-forms-and-charts/*

225 *Free Genealogy Forms and Charts - http://www.genealogysearch.org/free/forms.html*

226 *Charts and Forms from Ancestry.com*

- *- https://www.ancestry.com/cs/charts-and-forms*

227 *Free Ancestral eBooks - https://ancestralfindings.com/ebooks/?store=%2Fcategories%2Fancestral-findings*

THANK YOU FOR READING!

I would like to thank you for purchasing and reading this e-book or paperback. I hope you have found the information and material helpful in your family tree research.

If you enjoyed this book or found it useful I any way, I'd be very grateful if you could post a short review on Amazon. Your support really does make a difference and I read all the reviews personally so I can get your feedback and make this book even better. Please tell a friend so that this resource can find the right readers :-)

Thanks again for your support!

https://www.amazon.com/Steps-Researching-Your-Family-Tree-ebook/product-reviews/B07C5ZKB86/

OTHER BOOKS

Tormented by Ghosts – True Life Experiences

Author Lynda Bogert and Darrell Gibbs

Cover Illustration: JRC Dyer

ISBN: 978-1-77302-121-8 (Paperback)

978-1-77302-122-5 (eBook)

ASIN: B01I233XZA

Available:

Amazon - https://www.amazon.com/-/e/B01I233XZA

Kobo - https://store.kobobooks.com/en-ca

Indigo - https://www.chapters.indigo.ca/

Smashwords - https://www.smashwords.com

Barnes & Noble - http://www.barnesandnoble.com

EXCERPT FROM TORMENTED BY GHOSTS

Chapter 7 - The Old Funeral Home

Years ago I worked with a woman at the General Mills plant in Trenton, Ontario. Her name was Shelly and she was married to a well-known businessman in town.

She asked me one day to come over to her place for a tea. So I agreed. Her house was a huge and beautiful older Victorian home with original wood flooring. When I arrived, I felt a dreary dark gloomy presence. As soon as I stepped foot inside the feeling turned cold. I wasn't sure if I wanted to leave the large front entrance but not wanting to be rude I took my shoes off to enter. I looked to my left and saw the staircase and a beautiful dark oak banister. My eyes followed the banister up to the hallway where I saw an apparition of a woman.

As soon I saw her I felt my heart drop. I was hypnotized when our eyes locked onto each other's. Neither of us blinked.

"What the hell? Who is that?" The woman was not from this century.

Shelly said, "What are you seeing and what are you talking about?"

"Can you not see her?" I felt frenzied.

"No! Lynda, what is it?"

My breathing was getting harder and faster, like I was having a panic attack. The appearance of the ghostly woman was an unpleasant site as she had a cold miserable and mean stare. The first thing I noticed was her dark brown eyes and her eyebrows, looking disgusted. Her dark hair was up in a bun and she had white skin. The ghost was medium build and she appeared to be about 45 years old. She looked very prim and proper wearing a long Victorian dress with a collar up to her neck. The dress was snug around her waist and somewhat full looking. She had on old-fashioned boots with a bit of a high heel.

"Oh shit!" I muffled. I had sea sickness, but for some strange reason I was drawn to her face. I took several deep breaths to control my breathing to slowly walk upstairs. Shelly followed closely behind me as I was explaining to her about this woman standing in the hallway. I was terrified. I sensed she wanted to observe me closer. Normally, I would have run out the door and never return, but I felt the apparition was pulling me up the stairs towards her.

Shelly was freaking out. "Lynda, we don't have to do this. I'm scared!"

"So am I, Shelly." My body vibrated with fear. At the top of the stairs our eyes interlocked as I stood beside her.

"Is she still standing there?"

"Can you not see her? Tell me you can!"

Shelly looked terrified "No, Lynda, I can't see her." Her voice was shaky and filled of fear. Shelly stood near the top of the stairs but didn't get on to the top landing.

I turned and looked sideways at this woman more closely. She looked like she belonged in the 18th century.

Shelly then said, "There is a female ghost dressed in older clothes who keeps showing up, getting into my husband's face and scares him all the time."

"This is her!"

The ghost was a full apparition, but her body was not quite filled out. I was still looking into this ghost's face and she was looking at me. "You can stay here, but you cannot show yourself. You need to

leave Shelly's husband alone." I don't know what came over me to say this or even to walk up the stairs to confront her. It wasn't like me to do such a thing, but I did.

And like that, she vanished. I stood in melancholy solace "What have I done? I hope she is not going to do anything to us." We both ran downstairs. I felt like I was in a light trance and a bit disoriented.

Shelly explained to me what was going on in her house including strange noises and this female ghost scaring her husband.

I told Shelly that the house felt like an old funeral home built in the 18th century. She told me, "When I go upstairs to the bedrooms, I get a dreadful and uneasy feeling."

I had the same feeling and I didn't know why. I was feeling disconnected from myself; normally, that's not like me to walk up to a ghost and stare at one face to face. I realized what I had done afterwards."You are brave."

"I don't know what possessed me to do it." I stayed for a few minutes, but before I left , I said, "I hope your husband doesn't see that woman anymore. Another thing, I would be moving out of this house as soon as possible because I feel a lot of ghosts are here in this house. The house feels so intense, cold, and somewhat negative."

"I have had that feeling, too, but I wasn't sure."

I was scared for her and her husband. "Sorry, Shelly, but don't expect me to come back. I will see you at work, okay?" As we said our goodbyes, I gave her a hug.

I felt disoriented driving back home that evening. As soon as I got in, I did a spiritual cleansing, so I could get my faculties together and be safe.

Find out what happens next.

Goto

https://www.amazon.com/-/e/B01I233XZA

ABOUT DARRELL GIBBS

Author of '**22 STEPS IN RESEARCHING YOUR FAMILY TREE**'

Darrell was born in Korbecke, West Germany in 1956 – his father was in the Canadian Army stationed in Soest in northern part of the country. He grew up on army bases during the sixties and early seventies until his father retired. Darrell joined the Canadian Armed Forces in 1974 and was posted to various bases in Canada and was posted to Lahr, Germany for five years. Darrell retired after a successful career from the Canadian Armed Forces and the Public Service after 38 years as a *chef and kitchen manager*. He earned a diploma as a *Computer Technician* earning him the *Presidents Honour Award* at Sir Sanford Fleming College.

Darrell is the loving father of three children and five grandchildren. He has many hobbies such as reading, writing, playing guitar, woodworking, renovating, reading and collecting hockey memorabilia. Darrell is a die-hard Toronto Maple Leafs fan.

Darrell co-authored the book **TORMENTED BY GHOSTS – TRUE LIFE EXPERIENCES** with Lynda Bogert. After completing the book he began writing **WESSEX REIGN** which is a fictional historical book with paranormal themes. **WESSEX REIGN – A FICTIONAL ACCOUNT OF AN ANGLO-SAXON KING'S CHRONICLE** with a planned book release in 2019. Darrell has been researching the period so that readers will be consumed into the story with the many different characters in the book wanting more. **WESSEX REIGN** will be a part of a series called the **UNITED ENGLALAND SERIES**.

Find out more at:

www.darrellgibbs-author.com

Darrell Gibbs's Amazon Author page

https://www.amazon.com/Darrell-Gibbs/e/B07C65SH5T/

Printed in Great Britain
by Amazon